LOOK AHEAD

THE MEDIA

a guide to working in...

The Media

Jeremy Wallis

Heinemann LIBRARY

First published in Great Britain by Heinemann Library,
Halley Court, Jordan Hill, Oxford OX2 8EJ,
a division of Reed Educational and Professional Publishing Ltd.
Heinemann is a registered trademark of Reed Educational & Professional Publishing Ltd.

OXFORD MELBOURNE AUCKLAND
JOHANNESBURG BLANTYRE GABORONE
IBADAN PORTSMOUTH NH (USA) CHICAGO

Designed by Ambassador Design Ltd, Bristol.
Originated by Ambassador Litho, Bristol.
Printed in Hong Kong/China

ISBN 0 431 09481 0
05 04 03 02 01
10 9 8 7 6 5 4 3 2 1

British Library Cataloguing in Publication Data
Wallis, Jeremy
A guide to working in the media - (Look ahead)
1.Mass media - Vocational guidance - Great Britain
I. Title II.The media
302.2'3'02341

Acknowledgements
The Publishers would like to thank the following for permission to reproduce photographs: BBC/Jamie Reid, p. 26; Camera Press Ltd., p. 11; Carlton Television, pp. 20, 21; Colorific/Danny Sanchez/Shooting Star, p. 30b; John Walmsley, p. 35; Katz Pictures/John Angerson p. 19, /Richard Baker p. 24; Magnum Photos/ABBAS, p. 14; Mirrorpix, p. 9; Pinewood Studios Ltd., p. 30a; Rex Features, p. 46; Ronald Grant Archive, p. 28; Steenbeck, Inc., p. 33; Telegraph Colour Library/Martin Riedl, p. 38; The Bass Museum, p. 36; The Guardian, p. 44; Trevor Clifford, pp. 13, 16; Tudor Photography, p. 5.

Cover photograph reproduced with permission of Frank Spooner.

Our thanks to Joanna Dring, careers co-ordinator, Banbury school, Oxon for her help in the preparation of this book.

Every effort has been made to contact copyright holders of any material reproduced in this book. Any omissions will be rectified in subsequent printings if notice is given to the Publisher.

Contents

Technical words, jargon and specialist terms are explained in the glossary.

Working in the media

THE MEDIA

This book shows the range of careers available in the media. It identifies qualities and qualifications you need and paths to follow to realise your ambitions. It also shows connections with jobs in other fields.

Success might come after a training scheme or period of work placement, from graduate sponsorship, from sheer determination and persistence, and sometimes as a result of pure luck! As you'll see from the case studies, it's often a little of everything.

Be realistic. Acting, for example, might seem glamorous and exciting, but it is insecure and, except for the very few who do well, badly paid! Hopefully, this guide will help you recognize your strengths and so enable you to succeed.

What is the media?

From print to TV and the Internet, the media is about communication. The obvious form is the press and there is a huge selection of newspapers in Britain: from the nationals to regional dailies, evening papers, weeklies and free sheets. Magazines remain popular by meeting demand for an informative approach on anything from sport to organic gardening. Books are also incredibly popular, as their sales show. Publishing is a huge, enterprising area of work.

Broadcasting has a great influence on our daily lives. It relies on technology and good communicators, and is a showcase for creativity. There are openings across the spectrum, from computing to creative writing. The film industry offers a similar range of opportunities.

Over 8000 different periodicals are produced in Britain.

FACTS
The first daily newspaper in Britain was the *Daily Courant* in 1702.
Today, there are over 8000 different periodicals published in Britain alone!

The sheer scope of the media means there is demand for both technical and imaginative skills. There are careers open for good organizers, people who are patient and creative, for those who have an eye for detail and those who can see the 'big picture'.

New developments

Keeping up with media developments is exhausting! Each advance opens up a whole new world of opportunities. Digital television can cater for the individual viewer. There are already channels devoted to history, sport, geography, science fiction, news, music, natural science, home shopping, even old TV repeats. The potential of interactive viewing is only now being explored.

The Internet has expanded even more quickly. In its infancy, it has changed our understanding of 'the media'. For the first time we can participate in the information revolution as citizens as well as employees or consumers.

Are you right for the media?

Whatever the career you are aiming for, academic and technical qualifications demonstrate you are a serious candidate, but you need more than that. You must have team spirit and be quick-witted, ingenious and flexible: personal assets for even the most technical jobs. It helps to have a range of interests outside of your work. This shows you are a balanced individual.

You may be expected to work unsociable hours, for example public holidays; the Queen's Speech on Christmas Day might be recorded in advance, but someone has to operate the equipment on the day! As a journalist or part of a location film crew you may be expected to travel or spend time away from home.

Try to take an interest in concerns surrounding the media. Like many careers, working in the media is about more than just having a job. There are many issues: about freedom of expression, censorship and editorial liberty. Even those in practical trades are involved; printers, for example, have an honourable tradition of fighting censorship. With rights also come responsibilities. Journalists have a Code of Conduct designed to maintain professional standards, defend press freedom and protect against invasion of privacy.

Shooting the messenger

Governments often blame the messenger for the message; in Nazi Germany, books were burned and newspapers closed to control ideas. On average, one journalist a week is killed covering conflicts around the world. But ideas always flourish: in Soviet Russia, samizdat literature – secretly printed books and magazines – helped bring about changes that resulted in the collapse of the Eastern Bloc.

Types of contract

Many people are employed full-time in all fields: from advertising, accounts and management through to creative and technical posts in reporting, production and distribution. However, as you will see from the case studies, many people are employed as freelances. Pressure on budgets means this is likely to grow in the future.

Working freelance

A freelance is a self-employed person with skills and experience they can sell. Being self-employed means being your own boss, with your own rules and regulations. But there are downsides: no guaranteed regular income, sickness or holiday pay but an obligation to honour tax and National Insurance yourself. Employers who use freelances do not have to carry the costs of permanent employment such as holiday pay, sickness or maternity provision.

Getting the best from this book

First, read it. Many careers will not have occurred to you. You might see one you never realized existed. There is a lot of crossover within the media, and many sections have jobs in common. This book will also help you decide whether the media is right for you. Don't worry if it is not. There are opportunities outside the media, and it is never too late to change direction if you know where you want to go.

Working in newspapers

National and local papers all need **writers**, **editors**, **photographers**, **printers**, people to sell **advertising** and even **astrologers**.

Journalism is an obvious media career. **Reporters** have a hard-living image and, while reality is less romantic, journalism is never routine. A **journalist** must be calm and patient, able to dash out accurate copy to tight deadlines – today's news really is tomorrow's fish and chip paper!

To work for *The Sunday Times,* a journalist needs a National Council for the Training of Journalists (NCTJ) qualification, a degree or equivalent, to show commitment to journalism and have 'gumption'. University qualifications are less important to tabloids like the *Sun* and the *News of the World*, but reporters must be committed to journalism.

Graduate training

Several newspapers employ university or college leavers on graduate training schemes. In 1998, *The Sunday Times* attracted 3000 applicants for two places! The *Sun*'s graduate training scheme attracted 250 applicants in its first year.

The saying 'a picture speaks a thousand words' is true of photo-journalism. In the right place at the right time, **photographers** can create news themselves. Many reporters and photographers traditionally train with local or provincial newspapers before moving to larger circulation papers.

Journalists give their stories to the newsdesk. These stories are passed to the **chief news editor** and editors responsible for the different areas of the paper.

The newsroom of a national newspaper depends on the latest technology for all its communications.

So tell me again what an editor does...

According to the dictionary, an editor prepares the work of others: correcting errors, ensuring text is clear and so on. However, there are many kinds of editors.

A newspaper **editor** supervises the whole edition, deciding which reports to run, the front-page story, the newspaper's opinion on issues. They rely on **section editors**, for example **news editor**, **photographic editor**, **financial editor**.

A **commissioning editor** asks writers to produce articles. In book publishing, commissioning editors generate ideas for books and employ writers to write them.

Sub-editors correct grammar and spelling and ensure text fits the house style. In publishing, they are often called **copy editors**.

A **film editor** cuts and splices film into smooth-running sequences. The **sound editor** adds effects, cleans up voices and adjusts levels. On-line and off-line editors splice images on video. An **off-line editor** produces a rough cut and an Edit Decision List (EDL). The **on-line editor** compiles the programme from original tapes according to the EDL.

Obviously, different editors possess distinct skills and qualities.

Breaking the news

Local papers are mostly concerned with stories about their communities. With a small staff, reporters cover a range of subjects. Provincial papers, such as the *Yorkshire Post*, carry national and international stories, while emphasizing regional news. The national press divides more or less into two: papers with detailed stories from around the globe and those that emphasize celebrity and royalty stories.

Newspapers employ **correspondents** with knowledge of specific subjects such as sport, science or politics. Some gain this on the job; others are employed because of their good grasp of the topic.

Many stories carry the by-line (the name) of a journalist but you often see mysterious words or initials like Reuters, Press Association, AP. These are agencies that send reports and photographs 'down the wire'. Some offer specialist reporting, others have a multinational network of journalists.

There is a range of employment contracts, with full-time staff supplemented by freelances. A trainee journalist might start on a salary of less than £10,000 per year, but can expect to earn much more with experience and training.

CONSIDER THIS...

Similar skills are involved in:

- Speech writing
- Political research
- Academia
- Drama
- Promotional copywriting
- Press and public relations.

CONSIDER THIS...

- More than just newspapers and magazines are printed. Printing companies produce flyers, labels, packaging, calendars and diaries, pamphlets, posters and greetings cards and many more besides.
- Distribution and logistical management skills are vital to supermarkets, manufacturing, oil companies, food producers and wholesalers, motor vehicle manufacturers, importers and exporters.

Other jobs

Newspapers also employ people to sell **advertising**. Applicants need good telephone manners, a clear voice and be able to write quickly and accurately. Local papers like the *South London Press* have no educational requirements for staff, but they need people who can deal with deadlines and have the 'gift of the gab'. Media sales salaries start around £13,000 pa (per annum, or per year).

Liz – Trainee Journalist

I'm glad to have been able to highlight the plight of Britain's water vole population!

Liz Thomas is studying journalism at the London College of Printing. During the summer break, she did unpaid work experience at the *Yorkshire Post*.

We do work placements as part of the course, but I wanted extra experience. As I'm from West Yorkshire, I know the Yorkshire Post. I didn't have a connection – I just wrote to the editor with my CV.

I've worked with the Business Desk and the West Riding Newsdesk, and next week I'm going to Features. Some trainees work with an experienced colleague who acts as a mentor (a guide or instructor) but I shadow members of staff as they work. I've had a few stories printed, which I'm pleased about. I followed up a press release and did a short feature on the plight of Britain's water voles!

I'd like to work on a national paper but when I graduate, I'll look for a job on a local paper, to get a good grounding in reporting. I love journalism; every day is different.

Press conferences are often crowded affairs, hastily arranged following dramatic events. This press conference was convened in New Jersey, USA after the devastation caused by Hurricane Floyd.

Working in magazines

THE MEDIA

There are over 7000 magazines in the UK on everything from accountancy to zoology. Magazines thrive because people want specialist information, and demand is predicted to grow. **Consumer magazines** are well known but there are thousands of others.

Business and professional magazines cater for people in business such as grocers and builders, and for professionals such as architects and doctors. They advertise job vacancies and provide specialist news, often in technical language only easily understood by the target audience.

Reaching the target

Business magazines can target ads at the right audience perfectly. For example, a catering equipment manufacturer advertises in the hoteliers' and caterers' trade journal because these are the only people likely to buy the product. In 1997, adspend (spending on advertising) in consumer magazines stood at £583m, but adspend in business magazines topped £1018m!

Customer magazines, for customers of companies like Sainsbury's and Ford, are worth more than £330 million. *AA Magazine* has the highest magazine circulation in the UK – over 4 million.

Because of this demand for specialist knowledge, a journalism qualification is not always essential and magazines provide opportunities for people with other technical or professional qualifications. A **commissioning editor** may be more concerned that a writer can produce a feature on economic policy, or ride a mountain bike to destruction and survive to write the review.

Action shots add realism to any article or magazine cover.

The commissioning editor organizes contributions from specialist editors, staff and freelances. The **production editor** oversees origination and printing with **art directors** and **designers**. A technical editor or features editor could earn in excess of £25,000 pa, an experienced sub-editor over £20,000.

The production quality of consumer magazines – editorial, design and photography – is generally high. Many **photographers** concentrate on one category: fashion, cars, silverware, portraiture, even animals. They rarely work alone. Alongside are **stylists**, **hairdressers**, **make-up artists**, **photographic assistants** and **models**. A freelance photographer might charge over £450 per day, but may have very high overheads to cover.

Enthusiasm required

EMAP Active produces, among others, *Car, Total Sport* and *Trail.* Staff writers must have an interest in the subject, a journalistic qualification and writing ability. 'We're obsessed about our subjects and we like our journalists to be obsessed too!'

Designers should ideally have a qualification in magazine design. 'A good designer understands how words and pictures work together.'

This fashion shoot for Christian Lacroix involves hairdressers and many others beside the photographer.

Hey, good lookin'!

Not all models are slender and stylish: some make a living modelling hands or feet, or are just 'ordinary'. There's even an agency that specializes in 'ugly' models!

CONSIDER THIS....

SIMILAR SKILLS CAN ALSO BE USED FOR:

- INFORMATIONAL AND TECHNICAL AUTHORSHIP
- DATABASE MANAGEMENT
- MARKET RESEARCH
- PROMOTIONAL COPYWRITING
- COMMERCIAL PHOTOGRAPHY, INCLUDING WEDDING PHOTOGRAPHY, PORTRAITURE, INDUSTRIAL AND ARCHITECTURAL PHOTOGRAPHY, MEDICAL AND SCIENTIFIC PHOTOGRAPHY.

Because magazines sell pages to advertisers for thousands of pounds, **advertisement executives**, **promotions managers** and **account directors** are employed to maximize this income.

The **marketing and circulation staff** examine the market, target audience and competition to ensure each magazine reaches the right reader at the right price and that there is a market for any new title being launched. They also build databases, important for any magazine but vital to those distributed free and financed from advertizing. Marketing staff can earn anything from £22,000 to £50,000 pa.

John – Magazine Editor

My day starts with a cup of tea.

John Partridge edits a magazine published by a charity campaigning on social issues.

It's not possible to describe an average day; each is different, depending on where we are in the production cycle. This begins immediately after the publication of one issue, and ends with the publication of the next.

First we discuss what's going in the next issue then meet the editorial board, comprized of experts in the field and representatives of the charity, to get their views. We consider what's likely to be in the news – for example the Budget – and try to guess what might be announced.

We commission articles from freelance journalists, our own journalists and professionals such as Members of Parliament or other experts. Photographs are usually commissioned or picked from our photo-library or agencies. Agency pictures often come down the wire straight into our computers!

We edit the articles to fit the house style, correct grammatical errors, and make them the right length. During production week, we design and set text using QuarkXpress – a popular page design program. We send the pages we've done that day down the wires to the printers every evening.

By the end of the week the whole magazine has been printed and collated, and the first issues are sent to subscribers.

There are generally two ways into the profession: on a training scheme run by a magazine company or a course recognized by the Periodicals Training Council.

Advice from an insider

If you're interested in journalism, don't do Media Studies! Media Studies students don't specialize or write lots of articles and they can't compete for jobs with people who have studied journalism. If you don't want to study journalism immediately, it's better to specialize in a subject or field of study.

Working in publishing

Publishing is big business. Libraries and bookshops stock fiction and non-fiction: biographies, histories, language books and practical guides. There are thrillers, children's books and literary novels.

There are many stages between writer and reader. These stages form the core of the publishing business. A **publisher** must ensure there is a market for a proposed book, comparing it to similar titles, deciding how to sell it and who the buyers are likely to be. Successful publishers must recognize marketable books and, sometimes, marketable authors. They also manage their list of books, knowing when to reprint or drop a title, or commission a new title.

Libraries and bookshops stock fiction and non-fiction, covering everything from children's books to classics and beyond.

Judy – Book Illustrator

At the moment I'm drawing a cheese sandwich. It's not the most exciting piece of work I've ever done!

Judy Barnard is a freelance illustrator whose work has enhanced a large number of books.

I did Fine Art at university, and after a couple of years painting huge canvases for no money, a friend suggested I did illustrations. He gave me a few contacts and I sent samples of work to them.

A lot of my work is for publishers. I recently illustrated graphic versions of some of Shakespeare's plays aimed at 13–16 year olds. I got the commission quite out of the blue! I've also worked for magazines and advertising agencies.

I enjoy my work and there's plenty of it. In terms of income, it's difficult to give a figure. Some commissions pay more than others; advertising is excellent, but there's lots of competition!

In common with the rest of the media, publishers employ freelances, as **writers**, **researchers**, **designers**, **proofreaders**, **editors**, **illustrators** and **photographers**. Managing so many freelances is itself a challenge!

When an author delivers a commissioned title, the first task is to read and edit it, correcting errors of grammar and spelling. An **editor** may cut passages or entire sections if the manuscript is too long. Editing brings its own problems. Illustrated books combine text and images, but the editor is often dealing with words only. In **scientific, technical and medical** books the editor deals with complicated processes. Confusing the word 'pull' with 'push' in a guide to car mechanics is one thing; imagine the effect in a textbook on advanced heart surgery! An editor will often call on the services of an **expert reader** to verify the work.

The market

Publishing owes a lot to marketing, as novels of the `Aga-saga' genre show. (An Aga is an expensive stove which, so marketing people say, represents a lifestyle that many women aspire to or identify with.) Most of these novels have similar covers – serene summer scenes of green trees, floral dresses and straw hats – designed to appeal to women. Similarly, Nick Hornby's *Fever Pitch* was followed by many new books on sports themes.

Designers create the layout using computer programs like QuarkXpress. **Picture researchers** explore picture libraries for suitable images, or commission new ones from photographers and illustrators.

When design and layout have been completed and illustrations and photographs scanned in, the book is ready for production. Book printing is itself specialized, with distinct techniques of typography, colour reproduction, printing, collating and binding.

The publisher's work is not yet finished. Copyright protection, contracts, and selling the printing rights to other publishers all have legal implications. Legal knowledge is essential for senior publishing professionals as well as **in-house lawyers**.

Marketing, **publicity** and **promotions** are also crucial. Hodder Headline, a major publishing company, likes recruits to demonstrate a commitment to publishing. They prefer candidates to have completed some work experience, usually unpaid, during college breaks. Recruits come from a range of disciplines. There is no formal training scheme and the business is learned on the job.

Prominent book displays are important aids to help promote sales.

Another publisher, Random House, does not have an in-house training scheme either, but they are considering one. Most recruits are university graduates. A degree in English or Publishing helps but is not essential. Recruitment is less about qualifications and more about enthusiasm, a commitment to publishing, and initiative. Again, work experience in publishing or a related field really helps the applicant.

Most enter publishing as assistants, for example as **editorial assistants** or **production assistants**. Several publishers send staff on courses run, for example, by the Publishing Training Centre, Book House, in London, and by the London College of Printing.

CONSIDER THIS...

THE SKILLS THAT QUALIFY A PERSON FOR A CAREER IN PUBLISHING ALSO EQUIP THEM FOR:

- PUBLICATIONS DEPARTMENT OF A LARGE CHARITY OR OTHER NATIONAL ORGANIZATION
- LOCAL AUTHORITY OR GOVERNMENT BODY
- IN-HOUSE PUBLICATIONS FOR LARGE COMPANIES.

Many authors are represented by **literary agents** who try to get them the best deal from publishers. Agencies are often small, and few have formal training schemes. Tom, working for an agency in London, said, 'I came in as a **receptionist**: fielding telephone calls, photocopying, making tea. People get swamped with work and, if you show you're capable, they'll pass things on. Gradually you become more established as an **assistant** – talking to publishers, dealing with journalism pieces and short stories, selling material to foreign journals.'

Working in television

Broadcasting is big. The BBC employs 30,000 people, 20,000 work for the large independent broadcasting companies and thousands more work on one-off or fixed-term contracts, or for smaller independent programme makers. In 1998, Channel 4 spent £290m and commissioned work from 465 companies. BBC TV spent £1459m! For every person on screen, there are hundreds working behind the scenes.

Television provides chances to develop technical and creative skills, often in the same job. Competition is fierce: the BBC receives tens of thousands of unsolicited letters and CVs, and in one year there were 20,000 applicants for 300 trainee placements! Don't get downhearted: positions do exist and satellite and digital broadcasting mean yet more people are needed.

A news broadcast features **presenters** and **reporters**. Behind the scenes are **camera operators**, **sound engineers**, **floor managers**, **studio managers**, a **director**, **editors** and **researchers**. Because it's live, everything has to be right; news stories don't wait for a second take.

In any studio broadcast, there are more people behind the cameras than in front of them.

Some programmes are shot on location. Here a scene is being filmed inside a factory for Carlton TV's Peak Practice.

The tone of a holiday programme is different. Reports are carefully edited for maximum impact. 'Personality' presenters and good researchers are essential. **Foreign linguists** are an important part of the team.

Popular soaps like *EastEnders* need **writers**, **script editors**, **prop managers**, **set designers**, **carpenters**, **continuity managers**, **make-up artists** and **hairdressers**. And **actors**! Some programmes, like *The Bill*, are shot on location. Finding and managing good locations is a full-time job.

CONSIDER THIS...

SIMILAR SKILLS ARE NEEDED TO WRITE:

- FOR STAGE, RADIO OR FILM
- TRAINING VIDEOS FOR INDUSTRY AND COMMERCE
- ADVERTISING COPY
- PROMOTIONAL MATERIAL.

Weekly dramas are written, rehearsed and filmed quickly; a nature documentary might take months or years. The **producer** unites scientists, zoologists and naturalists with **technicians** using state of the art equipment.

Big-budget historical drama could not be produced without **writers**, **advisers**, **costumes**, **props, locations**, **visual effects**, even **catering**. In post-production, **editors** join scenes together and dialogue might be re-dubbed. Theme tunes will be composed and incidental music added.

All this represents just a few hours of television. There are five terrestrial broadcasters, transmitting 24 hours a day, plus many more satellite and digital channels.

Gary – Off-line Editor

I recently worked on a documentary and to finish on time, I had to set up an editing-suite in my dining room!

Gary Mason has been a freelance off-line editor for eight years. He makes editorial decisions with the director. Many off-line editors go on to become directors.

My interest started with drama, then making home movies with some mates. Before I went to college, I pestered my drama teacher to put me in touch with a film director he knew. I worked as an unpaid runner for two months – doing errands, dropping off videos, but mostly making tea!

I did Sociology and Politics A level, and studied Sociology and Communications at Goldsmiths' College in London. The course had a 25% practical element, which was perfect. As it was, I spent most of my time in the studio! I made a film at college that went on to win a prize.

After college I couldn't get work as an editor. I finally got a job as a runner – paid this time – and spent the next twelve months making tea again. I heard that a music programme needed a runner and talked my way in. By the end of the second series, I'd made myself useful (indispensable, really) and I made sure they knew I could edit. For the third series, they made me an editor.

I've built a good reputation among programme makers, so I'm never short of work.

There are drawbacks; the deadlines make for long hours so I end up living on curries and fries! But I wouldn't change my job. I love it!

Picture editing uses special computer facilities such as 'Lightworks'.

Opportunities in television

The **producer** coordinates each stage of a programme's development from origination, budgeting, the selection of writers and performers to rehearsals and filming. Producers need to be creative and organized. Many specialize, producing drama, wildlife or comedy programmes, for example.

Writers devise plots and compose scripts. They must be able to meet deadlines and work as part of a team. **Script editors** liaise between writers and producers, develop stories and guarantee writers portray characters consistently. **Researchers** confirm and prepare stories for broadcast. They might do interviews, provide briefings and find participants. Researchers often have a background in journalism. Trainee script editors can earn £13,500 pa, a researcher over £17,000.

> **CONSIDER THIS....**
> JOURNALISTS ALSO WORK FOR CEEFAX AND TELETEXT, AND PREPARE INFORMATION SERVICES ON THE INTERNET.

The **director** is in charge of a shoot and makes both technical and artistic decisions. Directors usually have a film school or theatre background and production experience. TV directors usually work from the control room, watching everything on monitors and communicating via the **floor manager**.

The job of **camera operator** demands an understanding of electronics and optics, good vision and a sense of picture composition. A single person normally operates each camera, sometimes with a **crew** to run gantry cranes, pull focus (focus the camera) and move cables. News camera operators often work alone, and frame shots, edit and service equipment themselves.

Sound technicians site microphones out of shot and ensure equipment works. In the control room, **sound mixers** adjust the balance, and feed in music and sound effects.

Electricians and **lighting console operators** set lights as instructed by the **lighting director**. Lighting for television demands a high degree of technical skill and artistic flair.

Creative and technical salaries are very dependent on experience. Because so many are employed as freelances, pay is good when working, but many can barely scratch a living between jobs. Be warned!

Everything from a drama to a chat show needs a set. This must look good but the **set designer** has cost and technical aspects to consider. Sets are built by **carpenters** and **joiners** and decorated by **scenic artists**. **Property (props) managers** look after movable items. **Props buyers** will purchase or hire anything from ingredients for a cookery show to a horse-drawn carriage for a drama.

Good visual effects help viewers suspend disbelief – where is the dramatic tension if Planet Earth is threatened only by a wobbly asteroid made of papier mache and chicken wire? **Special effects (f/x) technicians** also ensure that pyrotechnics and other effects look real but do not endanger actors or crew. Because **visual effects** is a broad category, one of the many specialist companies are commissioned for particular projects.

TV directors usually work from the control room, watching everything on monitors and communicating via the floor manager.

Jack of all trades...

As TV companies become more cost-conscious, location crews are shrinking. The emphasis is on multi-tasking, with each person doing several jobs. A presenter might research and direct; a camera operator might set up sound and lighting.

Make-up artists and **hairdressers** support the on-screen image – from powdering someone's shiny nose through to creating realistic scars and bruises.

CONSIDER THIS...

Make-up and hairdressing skills can also be used in:

- Hairdressing – salon work or self-employed
- Beauty salon work
- Health spas
- Make-up artist for a fashion photographer.

Costumiers design and tailor costumes or select from the **Wardrobe Department**. An applicant must understand fashion and its history, and be trained in theatrical design or fashion.

Production assistants support the director. They must remain calm under pressure, be exceptionally methodical, show initiative and work well with others. **Continuity assistants** guarantee consistency, noting details of set, props, clothes and the position of cameras. Forgotten particulars will stick out: imagine a Viking wearing a wristwatch or a woman in a hat that changes colour!

Location managers find suitable sites for filming. They secure permission for use, and guarantee the location is left as it was found.

Few of the jobs outlined above are first jobs – to aim for one you will need several years of successful and relevant experience.

Other careers in television

There is also demand within television for lawyers, accountants, marketing managers, sales people, computer experts, and individuals with management experience of retailing, IT, finance and leisure.

Working in radio

Technically, radio broadcasting is similar to TV. There are opportunities for **news editors**, **sound engineers** and **tape editors**, **producers**, **specialist presenters** and **continuity announcers**. **Correspondents** and **reporters** often switch between radio and television, and TV takes on many journalists already qualified in radio.

Radio journalists need the skills of a newspaper reporter, plus a few more, including the ability to edit material into a 'listenable' form. Though entrants still come from newspapers, most complete pre-entry courses at colleges approved by the Broadcast Journalism Training Council. **Sub-editors** are employed to write bulletins and scripts for stories and features. An experienced radio journalist working for a regional station can earn over £24,000 pa.

Radio 4 is a model of diversity. Daily schedules include **news** and **business** coverage, **short stories**, **plays, shipping forecasts**, **advice** and **consumer** programmes, shows covering **arts**, **science** and **comedy**, and a very long-running **soap** – *The Archers*. Radio 5 meanwhile has broadened the scope of sports reporting in Britain. Other stations broadcast music.

A live broadcast of the Radio One Roadshow *has two audiences – the live one at its venue and its listeners.*

Don't forget the World Service!

The BBC World Service broadcasts news and information in English and a variety of languages all around the world simultaneously on radio and the Internet. World Service audiences number over 143 million! For many people, the BBC World Service is their only source of news. The World Service employs fluent foreign linguists.

CONSIDER THIS...

The skills of a radio technician can also be used in:

- Hospital radio
- British Forces Posted Overseas radio
- Recording studios
- Live sound engineering
- Telemarketing
- Audio books services
- Translation services.

Local radio is very popular with listeners. Local stations produce quality documentaries, features of interest to their region and broadcast comprehensive news coverage as well as phone-ins and music shows.

Radio broadcasting, like magazines and multi-channel digital television, can cater for the diverse and increasingly sophisticated demands of listeners. Commercial stations have been established to satisfy particular tastes. A number of stations in major cities transmit information of consequence to ethnic minorities, often in their mother tongue. More radio broadcasters are now commissioning plays and documentaries from a growing number of **independent radio production companies**.

While BBC national and local radio is paid for through the licence fee, commercial stations depend on advertising revenue. Marketing departments sell the station's audience to local and national advertisers.

The employment of freelance staff and small production companies is a growing feature of radio today, but both BBC and independent radio train technicians and journalists. The BBC runs a two-year local radio trainee reporter scheme; there were 1500 applicants for fewer than 40 places in 1996!

Working in films

Lights! Cameras! Action! 'The film business is like a circus,' one insider reported. 'There are lots of strange characters in it.'

Film making shares many production techniques with television. There are technical differences (film instead of video) and differences in costs (most movies have larger budgets) but many jobs are similar. As a consequence there is some crossover of personnel between television and film, as well as advertising and promotional video making. The main differences are of scale. The **producer** of a BBC television programme is less concerned with pulling in the money from a number of different sources than the producer of an independent film. But both are involved in finding and developing stories and plots, engaging the right **director** and **actors** and other staff. The movie producer will also control schedules, publicity and other business matters.

Action movies like The Mosquito Coast *are often filmed in exotic locations.*

Hi diddle-dee! An actor's life for me!

Acting looks glamorous. Everybody has a favourite. A star can make a film; their absence can break it. Actors seem to live the life the rest of us can only dream about...

But it's time for a reality check: in 1999 Equity, the entertainment workers' union, found 29% of members it asked had done no entertainment-related work in the previous year. Many had simply given up. Of those working, only 20.5% had worked for more than 30 weeks in entertainment. 31.5% had worked between 11 and 30 weeks, and a massive 48% had worked for less than 11 weeks of the year.

In 1999, only 1% earned more than £50,000 a year and 24% earned nothing! 42% earned less than £5000. 12% earned £5000–£10,000, 10% earned between £10,000 and £20,000 and 5% earned between £20,000 and £50,000.

CONSIDER THIS...

FILM PRODUCTION SKILLS CAN QUALIFY YOU AS A:

- THEATRICAL MAKE-UP ARTIST
- THEATRICAL SPECIAL EFFECTS TECHNICIAN
- FIREWORKS DISPLAY TECHNICIAN
- DRAMA COACH
- TRAINING-FILM PRODUCER
- TEACHER
- EVENT MANAGER.

Filming involves **art directors**, **costumiers**, **construction teams and casting directors**. **Unit production managers** organize the shooting schedules for each day's filming plus details of everything needed – from actors to props, details of locations and costumes.

Over the last two decades, Britain's film industry has seen a renaissance. While domestically produced films are doing well, with an increase in the number made and their budgets, it is as a base for foreign film-makers – especially Americans – that is most lucrative. Britain is fortunate to have well-trained, talented and adaptable **technicians** and **visual effects artists**, good **actors**, and well-equipped studio complexes.

This tank at Pinewood Studios is very versatile and can be used for a variety of sets.

A cast of thousands...

The Phantom Menace involved over 600 people in special visual effects alone, including **animators**, **sculptors**, **make-up artists**, **draughts-people**, **model-makers**, **animatronic model designers**, **makers** and **operators**, **pyrotechnicians** and a **swordmaster**! There was also a *'***foley***'* crew creating sound effects, **editors**, **video editors**, **music coordinators**, **art directors** and **scenic artists**.

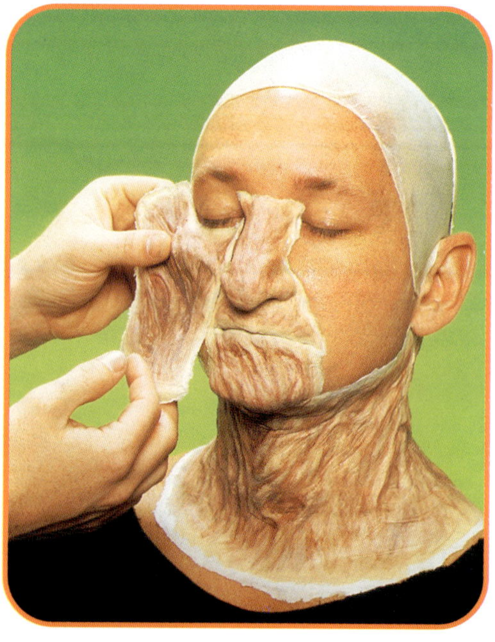

Special ***prosthetics*** *are applied to an actor's face to complete a monster makeover.*

Doug – Special Prosthetics Creator

I used to do a lot of decapitations, but they're all being done with computers now!

Doug Ellis specializes in a branch of visual effects that bridge the gap between make-up and special effects – creating special prosthetics for actors.

I'm dyslexic and at school I was drawn to art and creative things. I didn't know what I wanted to do after school, so I enrolled on a foundation course at Art College. I soon realized I wanted to work in film make-up and telephoned every studio in the South-east until one let me through the door. I proved I could make things and became a runner – buying materials, assisting the model-makers and make-up artists, and making the tea.

I worked on three or four films as a runner, and they let me do the messy model-making jobs no one else wanted. I watched and learned all the time on the job. There are courses, but I never found them necessary.

I learned that temperament is as important as talent. Skills can be learned but you either have enthusiasm and an easygoing character or you don't. I've built a reputation and done lots of sci-fi and fantasy films. My early work was horror – low-budget zombie movies!

Before shooting starts I spend a lot of time with the producer and director. Later we work closely with the actors who'll wear the prosthetics. Putting someone into a face mask or body suit can take hours, before even a single foot of film can be shot. And that means really early starts! In the evening it's all got to come off again.

When I take on a freelance, the first thing I ask myself is do I like them? It's important because of the close working relationship we all have on a movie. Then I ask for evidence of their skills, and what their strengths are – painting, sculpting, mould-making and so on.

The work is varied, and the challenges are always changing. Sometimes it's just plain weird; I've been shooting a movie about pixies, and I'm sitting in my workshop now, surrounded by buckets full of ears.

Post-production

Once the actual shooting of a film is completed, **post-production** follows – the stages footage must go through before it becomes a finished film. The principle tasks include **editing**, first the rough cut, then the fine cut, and **dubbing** on music, sound effects, re-recording dialogue, etc.

While production staff concentrate on finishing the film, another campaign is underway. If a film is to make money, people must pay to see it; so they must be persuaded that they want to see it.

During post-production an editor uses equipment similar to this Steenbeck editing table

CONSIDER THIS....

Interested in marketing and promotion? How about:

- Sales promotion
- Public relations
- Corporate sponsorship
- Media relations
- Cinema management
- Video sales and marketing
- Music sales and marketing
- Sales distribution?

The future is digital!

Effects created by digital technology and computer generated images have taken movies by storm. From the ground-breaking *Terminator 2: Judgement Day* and *Jurassic Park* to *Toy Story* and *Star Wars: The Phantom Menace,* digital effects have developed quickly. While the technology is costly, its price is falling all the time and it's likely that more film-makers will use it – and not just for jaw-dropping special effects. For example, an autumn sunset scene might be filmed at noon on a summer's day with the sunset and the autumnal scenery dropped in by computer later!

The next step will be to do away with film all together. Movies will be shot on digital cameras and shown in cinemas through digital projectors. Digital technology will also let new film-makers make pilots and films more cheaply than at present.

Distribution companies **promote** and **market** films in campaigns involving every medium – newspapers, magazines, television, the Internet. The intention is to create a buzz of expectancy that can only be satisfied by seeing the film. Some aspects of a campaign are obvious – press releases, advertising, interviews with director and stars, promotional photographs and trailers.

FACT

IN THE UNITED STATES, FILM FANS QUEUED AND PAID JUST TO SEE THE TRAILER FOR *THE PHANTOM MENACE.*

Other parts of the campaign are more crafty, such as planting stories on similar themes. For example, before *Silence of the Lambs* was released, newspapers carried serious features on serial murderers and cannibalism! Distribution companies must also ensure there are enough copies of the film to be shown in cinemas.

Merchandising is a lucrative industry in its own right. Toys, t-shirts, soundtrack CDs and other promotional materials are a valuable source of revenue. After cinema release, marketing departments will prepare and coordinate the launch of rental video and DVD (digital video disc), and the first television broadcast to ensure optimum coverage and maximize income.

Working in marketing

Once upon a time, marketing was something that large companies did. Now almost every type of organization is involved from companies and hospitals to health campaigns and charities. Growth means there is a demand for the right employees. But what do they do?

Marketing is about selling services or goods. It includes **sales promotion**, **market research**, **design**, **advertising** and **public relations (PR)**. Advertising and PR are covered in the following chapters. Marketing is anything which helps the seller sell.

In-house or agency?

Many organizations have in-house marketing departments staffed by their own employees. Others hire out-of-house agencies for their specialist knowledge. Agencies usually handle several clients at once; an **account manager** might promote beauty products to 19–28-year-old women one day and the next day help a charity fight child poverty. Each client requires different treatment, and the account manager needs to be good with people and be able to manage more than one project at a time.

Market researchers set out to discover things about customers: what they want, what they think about a product and how much they'll pay. This information can give a manufacturer or supplier the vital edge. While marketing is often seen as a creative business, accurate interpretation of market research data is critical, so **statisticians** and **mathematicians** are also in demand to analyse the data.

Market researchers interview members of the public to gather information.

New products are often tested on focus groups – groups of individuals chosen because they reflect the target market. Everything about a product is assessed, from colour and style to packaging and ideas for advertisements. Reactions are rarely straightforward, and **psychologists** are employed to work out what group members actually mean.

FACT

Ford named the Focus after the groups who played a part in its design and development.

What good is putting something in the shops if no one knows it's there? Advertisers liaise with **marketing managers** to ensure the right message is aimed at the right audience. Everyone needs to be convinced: wholesalers and retailers as well as customers. Sales promotion supports advertisements with free gifts, brochures, technical information and posters. At press launches, magazines and newspapers are encouraged to carry editorial copy. The marketing team oversees the process. Once excitement has been stirred up, the **sales department** must ensure stocks are high and the product is promoted in stores.

CONSIDER THIS...

Marketing skills can be used in a wide range of areas, including:

- Sales promotion
- Psychology
- Education
- Health awareness campaigns
- Event promotion
- Telemarketing.

Salaries in marketing range from £12,000 pa paid to graduate trainees to £50,000+ for a senior executive.

The hard sell...

Most bands or singers usually make an expensive video, which is an obvious crossover between TV, film and radio production. But the ultimate purpose of the video is to market a product – the record.

Working in advertising

Advertising is *the* hot, sexy career! Well not quite, and if any industry is criticized for being too cocky, it is advertising. In many ways this is unfair. Advertising insiders say they give consumers the information they need to make informed choices.

Advertising is a multi-billion pound business, employing teams of **planners**, **negotiators**, **artists**, **writers**, **production experts** and **coordinators** to create solutions for clients. What stands out about them is their range of backgrounds: arts and sciences are equally represented.

Advertising works

Tango sold 330,000 extra cans a day after introducing the 'big orange lad'! The makers of 'Wonderbra' had to build an extra factory to cope with demand after a poster campaign featuring supermodel Eva Herzigova.

Most advertising is in mainstream media – radio, television, newspapers, magazines and billboards. Other methods include point-of-sale (posters in shops), direct mail and direct marketing, and the new-tech media.

The Tango Man advertising campaign was highly successful.

Warning

A few words of warning if you are thinking about a career in advertising: applications to advertising agencies exceed posts by ten to one. Getting a job requires luck and persistence, and it helps if you have contacts in the industry.

Multinational agencies promote single brands worldwide with similar images and slogans. The smallest agencies depend on a single person devising campaigns and hiring freelance **designers**, **copywriters**, **producers**, **photographers** and **print buyers** as needed.

Large organizations offer clients a complete package – account management, planning and market research, media planning and buying, creative development, production, direct marketing, sales promotion and public relations.

CONSIDER THIS...

Similar talents and management abilities are utilized in:

- Sales
- Event management
- Campaigning
- Political lobbying
- Publicity
- Public relations
- Professional training
- Project management.

The **account manager** works on behalf of paying clients, explains the advertising brief to colleagues and the campaign team. A trainee account manager might earn £15,000 pa. Salaries paid to successful advertising professionals are generally high.

Agencies use **market research** to focus on the right audience, identified by age, sex, social class and interests. Briefed by the account manager, **account planners** and consumer researchers plan campaign strategy and decide which media to use. **Media planners** and **buyers** then buy advertising space in those magazines, newspapers and programmes whose audience profile matches the target.

Campaigns are planned under the guidance of the **creative director**. **Copywriters** draft text; the right wording is vital to stir up moods and appeal to the audience. In smaller agencies, the creative director is often directly involved in copywriting.

Jane – Account Manager

The hardest part of my job is keeping everything in the air – I feel like a world-class juggler!

Jane Smith studied Psychology at Durham University before deciding to work in advertising.

I wrote my thesis on subliminal advertising then took a second degree in Advertising at night school. I did work experience at two agencies and loved it!

My job is incredibly varied. I'm like the pivot on a see-saw. I help clients identify how advertising can help their business, then liaise between client and agency to produce the best advertising for their brands. In reality this means I might scout poster sites, suggest ideas for a story board, sit in on a voice-over session, or look over copywriter's drafts and the designer's roughs in the studio. And I must keep everybody happy.

An account manager needs good management skills and to be able to absorb lots of information fast. They also need energy and enthusiasm, good literacy and numeracy, a sense of humour and an appreciation of creativity. A second pair of hands might be useful, too.

A creative team discuss transparencies over a light box as they choose the best images for their campaign.

Poachers and gamekeepers...

Selling adspace is a crucial part of magazine, newspaper and broadcast income. While determined and confident media planners negotiate the best (cheapest) rates for ads, they are confronted by media sellers as determined to get the maximum revenue from their adspace.

People in advertising sales must be good presenters and negotiators, wise about the market and confident that the space they are selling offers better value than that of a competitor.

Art directors, with an art or design background, work with **graphic designers**, **illustrators**, the creative director and copywriters to create images and slogans or storyboards for TV adverts. **Agency producers** use these as the basis for ads and posters. Production values and costs are much higher per minute than most photo-shoots or films. Film-making skills are bought in, including well-known **film directors**, as well as **photographers**, **actors**, **voice-over artists** and **models**.

FACT

SEVERAL NOVELISTS HAVE WORKED AS COPYWRITERS. THE 'NAUGHTY BUT NICE' SLOGAN WAS COINED BY SALMAN RUSHDIE, AND 'GO TO WORK ON AN EGG!' IS ATTRIBUTED TO FAY WELDON.

Recruitment and training

While fewer than fifty agencies have structured graduate recruitment schemes, the larger ones take recruitment and training seriously. For example Saatchi and Saatchi, the big advertising agency, recruit 8–10 graduates from 2500 applicants into permanent posts bi-annually. They take graduates in a range of disciplines, but recruits must be committed to advertising and the advertising industry. Continued training is also encouraged for all staff. Most large agencies run similar schemes.

Working in public relations

According to the Institute of Public Relations, public relations, or PR, is a 'planned and sustained effort to establish and maintain goodwill and mutual understanding between an organization and its public'.

'Organization' means anything, large or small: a business, a charity or a government organization. An amateur theatre group sending a press release to a local paper to get publicity and improve the size of their audience is engaged in public relations. A large chemical company inviting Members of Parliament to visit a laboratory is engaged in public relations. A medical charity publishing its Annual Report is engaged in public relations.

Using the right photograph in a publicity campaign can make a real difference to its success. This picture was used in Spar's Childline appeal.

The 'public' is the audience: customers, employees, investors, the media, opinion-makers. To be effective, PR has to go two ways: organizations have to listen as well as talk. Over 48,000 people work in public relations in the UK today. Day-to-day activities might include report writing, issuing a press release, responding to a negative news story, writing an Annual Report, scripting a promotional video or video news release, organizing a stand for an exhibition, speaking at a public meeting or addressing members of the organization itself.

CONSIDER THIS...

THE PR SPECIALIST'S SKILLS ALSO EQUIP YOU TO BECOME A:

- PUBLICIST
- COPYWRITER
- MANAGER
- JOURNALIST
- CAMPAIGNS OFFICER
- EDITOR
- EVENTS MANAGER.

To confuse the issue, public relations departments operate under many different titles: Public Information, Public Affairs, Corporate Affairs, Customer Relations. However, they all have some role that is identified as public relations.

PR

As with marketing, there are two types of public relations operation. In-house departments devize and manage the PR strategy. Public relations consultancies provide advice to a range of clients and can devise and mange a PR strategy on their behalf.

Jobs in PR

The range of day-to-day activities in a PR department or consultancy gives a good idea of the jobs available, and the skills and qualities required of an employee.

Press officers needs to be familiar with the work of the organizations they represent, whether a charity, a business or a public body. They might be asked any number of questions, and if they don't know the answer then they must be able to find it quickly.

The PR person needs to develop good media relations, and have a good understanding of how the local and national press, television and radio operate, and what the special interests of individual journalists are. A junior PR officer might start on £12,000 pa. A more experienced senior press officer or manager can earn over £30,000.

From press release to news item

On page 11, Liz the trainee journalist explained that her water vole story had started when she followed up a press release. Many news items become stories like this; an organization or individual issues a press release to the newsdesk, editor or journalist who follow up the release and turn it into a story.

Writers and **editors** are vital in PR. The written word is the most important means of transmitting information, whether it is through reports, annual reviews, news releases, scripts, articles or features. Being an effective speaker is essential – on a one-to-one basis or to a large audience. An awareness of production and the ability to oversee the origination of brochures, reports, presentations, videos and films is important. Good event management skills are needed to direct news conferences, exhibitions, competitions and celebrations. Finally, research and evaluation skills are essential to help the modern PR agency or department assess how effective their work has been, and to help them develop their future strategy.

Cam-Wan – Press Officer

I make sure scientists explain things to me in language I can understand, and that makes it easier for me to explain it to the public.

Cam-Wan Lee is a Press Officer working for a large medical research organization.

I studied English at university, then spent a year working for the Students' Union. I'd worked on school and university magazines and this, combined with my experience at the Students' Union, helped me to get a job with a charity, working on their advice magazine.

I later moved sideways into the Press Office. I got in because of my journalistic skills and knowledge of the organization, but a number of colleagues had gone in first as unpaid volunteers or administration assistants, learning on the job before applying for vacant posts.

My day is very varied but usually I start by scanning all the daily papers – looking at the stories journalists have covered that we might be asked about. I take calls from correspondents who might be doing anything from asking about our latest research through to putting together an entire documentary. I write and prepare news releases and features for publication about new medical investigations, results and medical breakthroughs. To be honest, I seem to spend a lot of time on the phone!

Working in PR can be stressful and the hours erratic. It demands a lot of patience, persuasiveness and simple stubbornness. I once had to 'kill' a negative story from home early on a Sunday morning, to stop it running in all the papers the next day. I didn't have a chance to get out of my pyjamas until teatime!

New developments

Survival of the fittest?

Computers have brought about revolutionary changes in the way we study, work, communicate and play; their evolution is an opportunity for everyone. But they threaten the livelihood of many that cannot adapt. As the editor of *The Guardian* said of the Internet, 'I knew we had to link up or we'd be dead'.

The Internet

Most media outlets are now on the Internet, including the *Sun, The Times* and *The Independent. The Guardian* created *Guardian Unlimited*: a network of web sites, covering news, sport, jobs and careers, shopping and the arts. Integration with *The Guardian* newspaper lets users access background material on top stories. Over forty **journalists** and **designers** are employed. Launched in 1999, there were over 400,000 user registrations in the first year.

Newspapers produce web sites as well as their paper publications.

Andrew – Web-site Manager

Andrew Hodge is web-site Manager for a charity campaigning to end homelessness and poor housing in Britain.

I joined the charity as a temp (a temporary member of staff). I'd done English and History at University and was interested in communications and the media. When a permanent job came up I applied. I worked in various sections before getting this job. Marketing and Customer Services helped me in particular; as Web-site Manager I'm heavily involved in both.

My degree had a computing module but, to be honest, a deep understanding is not essential. My job is less 'techy' and more strategic: planning, responding to the demands and suggestions of users and the needs of the organization. It requires more 'media savvy' than an interest in hardware. But I do need to know what's going on and I'm involved in re-designing the web site.

Day-to-day responsibilities include updating information and putting up new pages. In the long term, we're looking at using the Internet to develop our image: what it can do as a communication tool, a fundraising tool, an educational tool. At the moment, we have 9000 users a month and that increases every month. Feedback mechanisms let people tell us what they think. Many ideas for the re-design were collected from users. For example, we get a lot of school students wanting info for projects; they want facts and figures, not boring policy documents. But at the same time we have to cater to decision-makers, professionals and potential supporters.

Everyone needs to be aware of the Internet; it grows massively every month as more people come on-line. The Internet is merging with TV, radio and communications. There are banking and e-commerce services. Some organizations no longer send out hard copy – a web site is cheaper.

This is a fantastic job; it's challenging, and I can get really evangelical about the Internet but it's the way of the future. And I'm excited being a part of it!

A paperless world of work?

Many organizations no longer mail out publications but refer enquirers to a web site. People interested in media careers will become increasingly dependent on Internet access for information.

The animated characters in The Phantom Menace *were created using computer-generated images.*

CONSIDER THIS...

If you're interested in IT, then how about a career as a:

- Web-site designer
- Software designer
- Computer engineer
- Games tester
- Network manager
- Graphic designer?

On-line sites like *Guardian Unlimited* have developed a user community. Users can register opinions, contribute to live chats with personalities such as the novelist Stephen King, and communicate with each other. The site has developed from an on-line version of the day's newspaper to a source of comment and information with its own identity.

A trainee web designer can earn over £15,000 pa, and a Webmaster in excess of £30,000.

Digital and computer technology

'I was in the right place at the right time, as technology moved from tape to non-linear computer editing', says Gary, **on-line editor**.

As seen already, new technology has already had an impact. Movies are being shot on digital cameras.

Traditional cut and splice **editing,** the work of the **camera crews** and **f/x techniques** are changing. Doug's work as a visual effects creator, described on page 31, has changed as a consequence of computer-generated effects. He has adjusted, but others have been less successful. The process is almost Darwinian, where only the adaptable prosper. Even actors are threatened: look at the animated characters in *Star Wars Episode One: The Phantom Menace*. Soon dead stars – Humphrey Bogart, River Phoenix, Marilyn Monroe – will walk the screens again, like computer-generated zombies!

CONSIDER THIS...

THE DEVELOPMENT OF INTERACTIVE TECHNOLOGY MEANS GROWING OPPORTUNITIES IN:

- INTERNET BANKING
- ON-LINE INSURANCE SALES
- CALL CENTRE STAFF
- E-COMMERCE
- COMPUTER SALES.

Television can now gives viewers a choice of viewpoints of the same event. Lightweight satellite technology has changed foreign reports, enhancing coverage of stories from around the globe. Radio broadcasting benefits from new technology: for example, telephone interviews conducted down ISDN lines are of higher quality than those conducted on regular telephone lines. Press photographers can transmit pictures via a modem; the photo of a match-winning goal can be on the screen of a page-making computer within seconds of being scored!

These represent new breaks for **technicians, editors, camera operators,** and other studio and outside-broadcast personnel. Staff must be flexible, and there is the likelihood of more multi-tasking.

Future perfect?

As Andrew said (page 45), the future is a fully-integrated media linking Internet, television, radio, communications, newspapers and magazines. Banking and e-commerce means we can buy products and services, book holidays, send e-mails. New technology represents an enormous range of career opportunities for people ready to take advantage of it.

Getting into the media

What qualities make a successful candidate?

People in all areas of the media repeatedly describe certain qualities: **enthusiasm**, **energy**, **commitment**. These, more than anything else, are characteristics that seem most desirable. Academic qualifications are still important, demonstrating intelligence and understanding, but you must show you are the right person for the job: one who is eager, hard working, resolute!

Commitment

Many of our case studies began their careers low in the pecking order, as volunteers and temps, post-room workers, runners and helpers. They made an impression by being thoughtful, co-operative and efficient: making themselves – as Gary explained – indispensable. They also made sure they were in the right place at the right time. They had an idea of what they wanted to do and set their sights on it: Doug telephoned every studio in the South-east, Gary worked as an unpaid runner, Jane did work experience, Cam-Wan worked on school and college magazines. They all did that bit extra – and they were willing to take risks.

Energy

Few jobs in the media can be described as nine-to-five. If a shoot starts at 7.00 am and actors need to spend two hours in make-up putting on prosthetics, do the maths and ask yourself: is this the job for me? A delay of just a few minutes because of technical problems will keep people waiting and cost money. Will you take responsibility and make sure it doesn't happen?

Ten minutes before the news is due to be broadcast, details of a major earthquake in southern Europe break – can you write a report in those few seconds, brief the newscasters, change the running order and pull a less important story calmly and without panic? Would you spend all Sunday on the phone stopping a story? Can you write accurate and effective copy for the late edition? Do you know your subject and feel able to write persuasive copy? If the answer to these questions is no, then perhaps a career in the media is not for you.

Enthusiasm: the future starts now!

Everything helps. Below there are some of the subjects you may study at school, and just a few of the media careers they are relevant to:

English

- Journalist
- Editor
- Researcher
- Press officer

The media is all about communication; a good level of literacy is important throughout. However, Doug's account, on page 31, of his dyslexia shows how commitment and choosing the right area, can overcome even this obstacle!

Science (especially physics)

- Camera operator
- Film/video editor
- Lighting technician
- Science correspondent
- Visual effects technician
- Scientific documentary producer/production assistant

Art and design

- Designer
- Art director
- Make-up artist
- Prosthetics creator
- Illustrator
- Set designer
- Photographer

Business studies and Economics

- Producer
- Journalist
- Distribution manager
- Market researcher
- Media planner/buyer
- Advertising sales executive

Maths

- Accountant
- Producer
- Project manager
- Production assistant

Good numeracy is essential for many technical jobs.

Drama

- Director
- Set designer
- Stage manager
- Lighting director
- Floor assistant
- Costumier

Fashion and design

- Costumier
- Hairdresser
- Make-up artist
- Props manager

History

- Researcher
- Historical adviser
- Journalist
- Writer

Politics

- Journalist
- Sub-editor
- Researcher
- Commissioning editor

Technical design

- Set designer
- Layout artist
- Lighting designer
- Art director

IT and Computing

- Web-site manager
- Animator
- Printer
- Computer-generated effects technician
- Journalist
- Editor

Computer skills are becoming more important every day throughout the media.

Geography

- Journalist
- Weather reporter
- Travel writer
- Environmental correspondent

Foreign languages

- Sub-titles writer
- Foreign correspondent
- Translator
- Travel programme researcher

Psychology/Sociology

- Market researcher
- Marketing executive
- Strategic planner
- Press officer

There are also a number of GNVQ courses designed to give vocational training and qualifications. These are examined in more detail in the next chapter.

Enthusiasm, energy, commitment

It's up to you! A career in any branch of the media is challenging. It is not always brilliantly paid, and with so many freelance contracts it can be precarious. However, it is clear how much each case study in this book enjoys their occupation. There are few fields of work that offer such obvious job satisfaction.

Useful information, addresses & contacts

Useful publications and journals

Many quality dailies have supplements with media jobs, and there are several trade magazines: *PR Week, Marketing, Marketing Week, Media Week, The UK Press Gazette, Campaign, Broadcast, Journalist.*

Further education and university courses

A degree is a good first option. It does not have to be media related. Employers often look for a range of interests. There are shorter postgraduate media courses you can take. Several bodies maintain training standards; many colleges and universities run media-related courses, but check with training authorities for lists of approved courses. Because placements are an opportunity to show what you can do, ensure courses have a good record for placing students.

Vocational courses

General National Vocational Qualifications (GNVQs) develop knowledge, skills and understanding of broad work areas. Most GNVQs are college based. **Intermediate GNVQs** are equivalent to four GCSEs at grades A*–C. **Advanced GNVQs** are aimed at 16–19 year olds. GNVQs relevant to media careers are:

- GNVQ Media: Communication and Production
- GNVQ Performing Arts and Entertainment Industries
- GNVQ Art and Design.

Also: IT, Business or Retail and Distributive Services.

National Vocational Qualifications or **Scottish Vocational Qualifications** are job-specific and can be followed to professional levels. NVQs are supervized by the Qualifications and Curriculum Authority (QCA).

Within NVQ Communicating, options include: Art Direction, Broadcast Engineering, Broadcast Journalism, Camera Assistance, Camera Operation, Costume Design, Administration, Design, Desk Top Publication, Editing: Post Production Support, Editing: Film Support, Lighting Direction, Photography, Production, Sound Assistance, Vision Control.

Training and Enterprise Councils (TECs) and **Local Enterprise Companies (LECs)** in Scotland deliver NVQ/SVQs in partnership with local employers.

National Traineeships and Modern Apprenticeships help school leavers gain skills and qualifications while working. National Traineeships offer training to NVQ Level 2 in Business Administration, IT, Photography, Telecommunications, and Electronics. Modern Apprenticeships take trainees to NVQ Level 3/4. Other exams including City and Guilds. Media-relevant courses include: Arts and Entertainment, IT, Newspapers (including Journalism), Printing (including Design and Layout), Periodicals, Telecommunications, Electronics, Broadcasting and Photography.

GNVQ, GCSE, A Level and NVQ units can be mixed.

BTEC courses are administered by the Edexcel Foundation. Media-related subjects include Web Site Design, Printing, IT and Computing, Animation, Sound Production and Editing, and Video Post-production and Editing. BTEC courses can be followed to Higher National Diploma level. For information on BTEC courses visit the Edexcel web site (see page 57).

You will find lots of information in your school's Careers Library. Course lists can also be obtained from QCA Publications or the QCA web site (see page 57). More information can be found on the DFEE web site, from the Training Information Service, your local TEC/LEC and Careers Service.

Journalism: pre-entry courses

Most trainees get jobs after full-time courses. This is **pre-entry** training. Look for courses approved by the National Council for the Training of Journalists (NCTJ), the Broadcast Journalism Training Council (BJTC), the Periodicals Training Council, the Institute of Public Relations (IPR) and the Communication Advertizing and Marketing Education Foundation Ltd (CAM Foundation). The National Union of Journalists recognize any course approved by these organizations. Courses fall into three basic types:

- **Access courses:** basic training to help students into open pre-entry courses.
- **Open pre-entry courses:** courses taken before you enter the profession. These include **degree** courses.
- **Postgraduate pre-entry courses.**

Courses contain practical training, work placements and a fair record of students finding work. (Fair record means few guarantee a job.) Colleges prefer applicants to do work experience before they begin. (The NCTJ offer a tip: avoid June or July, when lots of others are doing work experience as well!)

Journalism: direct entry courses

Direct entry courses are run by newspapers. Modern Apprenticeships fall into this category. Some publishing companies also run training schemes. Direct entrants attend block or day-release courses at college, and take the NCTJ's **National Certificate** or a **National (Scottish) Vocational Qualification** at level 4. Apply to the editor of a regional or local newspaper for employment as a trainee reporter or photographer.

Photojournalists train as reporters. Obviously energy, enthusiasm and commitment are needed, as well as a good eye for things that set an image apart. A list of approved courses is available from NCTJ.

Broadcast journalism

The Broadcast Journalism Training Council gives advice on careers in broadcast journalism. The BJTC maintains training standards. Graduate and postgraduate courses include:

- **Broadcast journalism** – mainly radio. (May include TV, but not to examination standard.)
- **Multimedia journalism** – broad-based courses which encompass television and/or radio.
- **Bi-media (Radio and TV) journalism** – training in radio and TV to examination standard.
- **Television journalism – pre-entry TV training.** Course content includes journalism, camera work, editing, the journalist and the law, script writing and documentary making. The BJTC say a degree is becoming more necessary for a career in journalism, but they list enthusiasm, energy and commitment as essential qualities. Course details are available from BJTC.

Magazine training

The Periodicals Training Council accredit training courses that produce multi-skilled staff. Many include work placements, and the PTC issues guidelines to maintain standards. Students organize their own placement. The PTC publishes a careers guide that includes journalism courses and a directory of magazine companies.

Film and television

SKILLSET, the National Training Organization for Broadcast Film, Video and Multimedia, produce material about careers and courses. Useful information can be found in *The Skillset Careers Handbook* or on their web site (see page 58).

You can find details of local workshops and courses from Regional Arts Boards and Film Councils.
The British Film Institute *Film and TV Handbook* contains information as well as contacts and addresses.

The Media Guide published by Guardian Books contains addresses, and overviews of areas including the BBC, ITV, C4 and C5, satellite and cable channels. The National Film and Television School run courses in all aspects of film and television. The London International Film School also run courses for film makers.

Marketing, public relations advertizing

Careers information is available from the Institute of Direct Marketing, the Institute of Public Relations and the Institute of Practitioners in Advertising. These and other organizations established the Communication Advertising and Marketing Education Foundation, (CAM Foundation) to administer examinations. The structure of CAM qualifications is now in line with the QCA National Framework. Individual advertising agencies also provide training, supported by the IPA.

Getting your foot in the door

Skillset offers advice about work placements applicable throughout the media. Many people apply for work placements: but placements go to the candidates who offer something in return. Always highlight competence and personal qualities as well as relevant experience:

- Keyboard skills, office skills, communication skills, writing, driving, organization, teamwork.
- Show you're prepared to work long hours.
- Be flexible.
- Send evidence of your talent and abilities.
- Remember the mantra: **enthusiasm**, **energy**, **commitment**.

Finally, learn how to make a good cup of tea or coffee. Reading through the case studies, it seems it is the first job anyone gets!

Useful addresses

For further information contact the organizations listed below. Most have web-site addresses.

Qualifications and Curriculum Authority
29 Bolton Street
London W1Y 7PD
Tel: 020 7509 5556 (Enquiry line)
www.qca.org.uk

For Northern Ireland:
QCA – NI
2nd Floor
Glendinning House
6 Murray Street
Belfast BT1 6DN
Tel: 028 9033 0706

Accac/QCA Authority for Wales
Castle Building
Womanby Street
Cardiff CF1 9SX
Tel: 029 2037 5400

QCA Publications
PO Box 99
Sudbury
Suffolk CO10 6SN
Tel: 01787 88444

Scottish Qualifications Authority
Hanover House
24 Douglas Street
Glasgow G2 7NQ
Tel: 0141 248 7900
www.sca.org.uk

For information on the National Traineeships and the Modern Apprenticeships contact your local Careers Service or **Training and Enterprise Council,** or:

The Training for Young People Division
Department for Education and Employment
Room W4D
Moorfoot
Sheffield S1 4PQ
Tel: 0114 259 3573
www.open.gov.uk/dfee/ntrintro.htm
www.open.gov.uk/dfee/mapintro.htm
Or contact:

Training Information Service
PO Box 200
Timothy's Bridge Road
Stratford-Upon-Avon CV37 9HY
Tel: 0345 66 55 88

Edexcel Foundation (BTEC)
Stewart House
32 Russell Square
London WC1B 5DN
Tel: 020 7393 4500
www.edexcel/org.uk

Magazine and newspaper journalism, broadcast journalism

Broadcast Journalism Training Council
39 Westbourne Gardens
London W2 5NR
Tel: 020 7727 9522
www.bjtc.org.uk/

National Council for the Training of Journalists Limited
Latton Bush Centre
Southern Way
Harlow
Essex CM18 7BL
Tel: 01279 430009
www.itecharlow.co.uk/nctj/

National Extension College
18 Brooklands Avenue
Cambridge CB2 2HN
Tel: 01223 450200
www.nec.ac.uk

Periodicals Training Council
Queens House
55-56 Lincoln's Inn Fields
London WC2A 3LJ
Tel: 020 7404 4168
www.ppa.co.uk

National Union of Journalists
Acorn House
314-320 Gray's Inn Road
London WC1X 8DP
Tel: 020 7278 7916
www.gn.apc.org/media/nuj.html

Other useful addresses:

Bureau of Freelance Photographers
Focus House
497 Green Lanes,
London N13 4BP
Tel: 020 8882 3315

Community Radio Association
The Media Centre
15 Paternoster Row
Sheffield S1 2BX
Tel: 0114 279 5219

Publishing

Publishing Training Centre
Book House
45 East Hill
Wandsworth
London SW18 2QZ
Tel: 020 8874 2718
www.train4publishing.co.uk

Film and television

SKILLSET
91-101 Oxford Street
London W1R 1RA
Tel: 020 7534 5300
www/skillset.org

National Film and Television School
Beaconsfield Studios
Station Road
Beaconsfield HP9 1LG
Tel: 01494 671234
www.nftsfilm-tv.ac.uk

The London International Film School
24 Shelton Street
London WC2H 9HP
Tel: 020 7836 9642/020 7240 0168
www.lifs.org.uk

BBC Recruitment Services
PO Box 7000
London W12 8GJ

BBC Careers Information operates an interactive careers telephone system as well as a complete web site guide to careers with the BBC.
Careers Information line: 020 8576 0639
www.bbc.co.uk/jobs

Independent Television Network Centre
200 Gray's Inn Road
London WC1X 8HF
Tel: 020 7843 8077
www.itv.co.uk

Cyfle: Gronant
Penrallt Isaf
Caernarfon
Gwynedd LL55 1NS
Tel: 01286 671000
www.cyfle.co.uk

Provides training for Welsh speaking technicians.

Other useful addresses

British Film Institute
21 Stephen Street
London W1P 2LN
Tel: 020 7255 1444
www.bfi.org.uk

Regional arts boards share a web site with a menu system for each Arts Board.
www.arts.org.uk

Eastern Arts Board
Cherry Hinton Hall
Cherry Hinton Road
Cambridge CB1 4DW
Tel: 01223 215355

East Midlands Arts Board
Mountfields House
Epinal Way
Loughborough LE11 0QE
Tel: 01509 218292

London Arts Board
Elme House
133 Long Acre
London WC2E 9AF
Tel: 020 7240 1313

Northern Arts Board
10 Osborne Terrace
Jesmond
Newcastle-upon-Tyne NE2 1NZ
Tel: 0191 281 6334

North West Arts Board
Manchester House
Manchester M3 3AB
Tel: 0161 834 6644

Southern Arts Board
13 St Clement Street
Winchester
Hants. SO23 9DQ
Tel: 01962 855099

South East Arts Board
10 Mount Ephraim,
Tunbridge Wells
Kent TN4 8AS
Tel: 01892 515210

South West Arts Board
Bradninch Place
Gandy Street
Exeter EX4 3LS
Tel: 01392 218188

West Midlands Arts Board
82 Granville Street
Birmingham B1 2LH
Tel: 0121 631 3121

Yorkshire and Humberside Arts Board
21 Bond Street
Dewsbury WF13 1AX
Tel: 01924 455555

Arts Council of England
14 Great Peter Street
London SW1P 3NQ
Tel: 020 7333 0100
www.artscouncil.org.uk

Arts Council of Northern Ireland
185 Stranmillis Road
Belfast BT9 5DU
Tel: 028 9038 5200
www.artscouncil-ni.org

Scottish Arts Council
12 Manor Place
Edinburgh EH3 7DD
Tel: 0131 226 6051
www.sac.org.uk

Arts Council of Wales
9 Museum Place
Cardiff CF10 3NX
Tel: 029 2037 6500
www.ccc-acw.org.uk

London Film and Video Development Agency
114 Whitefield Street
London W10 5RW
Tel: 020 7383 7755
www.lfvda.demon.co.uk

Northern Ireland Film Commission
21 Ormeau Avenue
Belfast BT2 8HD
Tel: 028 9023 2444
www.nifc.co.uk

Scottish Screen
249 West George Street
Glasgow G2 4QE
Tel: 0141 302 1700
www.scottishscreen.com

Sgrin, Media Agency for Wales
The Bank
10 Mount Stuart Square
Cardiff Bay
Cardiff CF10 5EE
Tel: 029 2033 3300
www.sgrinwales.demon.co.uk

Broadcasting, Entertainment, Cinematograph and Theatre Union
111 Wardour Street
London W1
Tel: 020 7437 8506

Marketing, public relations and advertising

Communication Advertising and Marketing Education Foundation Ltd (CAM)
Abford House
15 Wilton Road
London SW1V 1NJ
Tel: 020 7828 7506
www.camfoundation.com

Institute of Direct Marketing
1 Park Road
Teddington
Middlesex TW11 0AR
Tel: 020 8977 5705
www.theidm.com

Institute of Public Relations
The Old Trading House
15 Northburgh Street
London EC1V OPR
Tel: 020 7253 5151
www.ipr.org.uk/careers

Institute of Practitioners in Advertising
44 Belgrave Square
London SW1X 8QS
Tel: 020 7235 7020
www.ipa.co.uk

The Advertising Association
Abford House
15 Wilton Road
London SW1V 1NJ
Tel: 020 7828 4831
www.adassoc.org.uk

Get the jargon – a glossary of media terms

access course college course giving a basic grounding in a subject before more advanced study

account management/planning in advertising, marketing and public relations – dealing with everything to do with a single client or campaign

accredited training courses recommended or approved by an industry

adspace proportion of a magazine or newspaper that is available for advertising

brief (in advertising, PR and marketing) instructions about a campaign's aims laid down to the creative team

brief (in journalism) instructions to a reporter on a story to be covered

budget money allocated for the production of a film, TV programme, magazine, book or advertising campaign

Ceefax/Teletext news and information text service, piggybacking on television signals and decoded by suitable television sets

censorship control of news and information, images and words, by government, pressure group or media proprietor

copy text in an editorial story or advert

correspondent reporter with specialist knowledge

creative team team in an advertising agency responsible for the ideas, visuals and copy for a campaign

curriculum vitae (CV) detailed summary of a candidate's qualifications, previous jobs, experience and interests sent to prospective employer

Darwinian theory of evolution developed by Charles Darwin: those who are able to adapt to changing conditions stand the best chance of survival. Often used to describe situations where people must be flexible to cope with rapid changes.

database information about consumers and customers. Databases allow companies to target adverts and products very precisely.

digital broadcasting use of computer technology to transmit information to produce better reception, allowing more material to be carried than ordinary radio waves

digital technology computer technology now widely used throughout the media

direct marketing mailing or otherwise delivering information direct to consumers

down the wire sending or receiving text or photographs by modem through telephone wires

e-commerce buying and selling on the Internet – from stocks and shares to holidays and groceries

editor person responsible for ensuring work is ready for publication or broadcast

editorial freedom freedom of a newspaper/magazine to say what it wants without interference from the state or owner

feature in-depth look at a topic or issue

file submit a story to the newsdesk

fine cut last stages of film editing

foley sound effects on film

freedom of expression right of journalists and editors to express their views without interference

freedom of speech see freedom of expression

freelance self-employed person selling their skills on short-term contracts

f/x special effects

genre categories of fiction, such as thriller, horror, sci-fi

graduate person who has successfully completed a university or college degree

interactive technology allowing the consumer to participate rather than simply absorb information

Internet worldwide network linking computers

ISDN line digital land line

make up use of computer technology to create pages and printing films. Part of the printing process

market research examination of consumers' expectations, aspirations and opinions on products and services

marketing strategy the plan used to sell a product

media planning/buying and selling strategic planning of adverts, and subsequent negotiation between media buyers and those selling adspace

mentoring training of a newcomer by working alongside a more experienced colleague

multimedia the developing trend towards integrated media

multi-tasking Training individuals to take a number of different roles and responsibilities

National Insurance (NI) money deducted from a person's wages or salary by the state to cover them for sickness and unemployment benefits, pensions, etc

news agency/wire service company selling stories to the media.

newsdesk editorial room where news is prepared for publication or broadcast

non-linear editing video editing using computers that allows the editor to do away with videotape

overheads costs that have to be paid by a freelance or company from the fees they earn for a job. For example, a photographer must buy camera equipment and film and pay for studio space, photo processing, etc.

pilots and show-reels short films, shot as cheaply as possible, that show off the skills of film makers, directors, script writers

postgraduate training or a degree taken after completing a first degree at college or university

press release news story put out by an organization or individual to the media

product placement paying to have identifiable products or logos in a film or TV production

production all the stages of putting together a magazine, film, book, etc

proof reading examining text for mistakes

prosthetics flexible material applied to actors' faces to change thier appearance

renaissance literally, rebirth. Renaissance refers to the rebirth of culture, science and art in medieval Italy, but nowadays we use it to describe any great explosion of artistic action after a period of inactivity or contraction.

rough cut early stages of the film editing process.

runner person to run errands, sometimes called a 'gopher': i.e. 'go for this... go for that'

rushes raw film footage before editing

scanning in using a scanner and computer to place a picture, or piece of text onto a page

sourced obtained from

splice, cut and splice editing film by sticking sections of film together to make complete sequences

subbing to sub-edit (to ensure that correct grammar and spelling is used)

target audience the readers a publication is intended for

user community groups of users communicating with each other round an Internet site

vocational training job-specific training

Index